EX·LIBRIS

CARACTACVS

VENTA·ICENORVM

CONSVASOR·IMPERIVM

VORTIGERN

AMBROSIVS

VTHER

WORD HUNTERS

TOP SECRET FILES

A Compendium of Devices and Methods,
Compiled by Caractacus of Northwic,
with the aid of several hunters

NICK EARLS & TERRY WHIDBORNE
For your eyes only!!!

UQP

Dear Nick and Terry,

Once again may I say it was a pleasure to meet you on your visit to our school today. If only we had known in advance how many sandwiches you would eat, we would have had the tuckshop working overtime.

Occasionally citizens are called upon to perform a higher duty, and now I am calling upon you. In strictest confidence, I tell you that there is a dictionary, of a special kind, which holds the English language in its keep. It is the device we word hunter types use to travel when and where we need, to protect the very language that provides your livelihood. It is the product of meticulous research across thousands of years, all of it logged by Caractacus, the master of the dictionary, in his notebooks. He holds onto these books in the past, but often it is not safe there (and I don't just mean the toilets!). So I have brought one to our time for safekeeping and now, with library renovations ongoing and no secure place for it, I entrust it to you, men of the English language and the pictures that go with it!

14A.

It contains many fascinating facts brought by word hunters
to Caractacus, including the instructions to make a wonderful
suit of armour, the peculiar scoring system of the game now
known as tennis, and stories of language lost and found.
It also contains a log of three word hunter quests into
the past, though these are incomplete and we need your
writerly and picturely assistance to save these words.

Please take great care of this notebook. You mentioned your
publishing company, the University of Queensland Press.
Please hide this book in their special vault you told me
about — the one with the python. And make certain no one sees
it! Most of all, make sure it is never published!

Yours in Words,

Mursili Bogazkale
Deputy Librarian (Acting),
Cubberla Creek State School (2012AD —)
Formerly Supreme Librarian to the Royal Court
of Suppiluliuma II and the Empire of Hatti (1184 — 1180BC)

NOTES ON THE POPULAR GAME OF

~~JEU DE PAUME~~ ~~TENEZ~~
~~TENNIS~~ ~~SPHAIRISTIKE~~

TENNIS

Not according to Major Walter Clopton Wingfield!

Al

fig 1

fig 2

fig 3

It started out as a racquetless game played by French knights, but did they call it tennis? No. They called it 'la paume' (the palm) or 'jeu de paume' (game of the palm), since they played it with their hands. So, tell me hunters, how did it get the name 'tennis'?

Caractacus

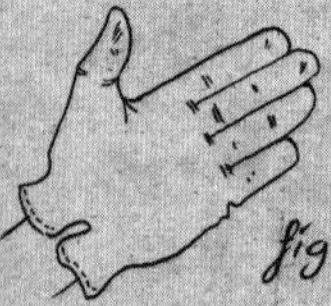

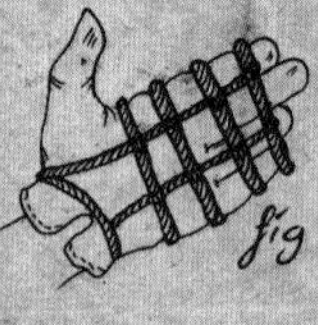

During the game, to get the receiver's attention, the server would call out 'tenez', which meant hold or receive. Apparently, people nearby heard that call and the game came to be identified by it. By the mid-13th century, 'tenez' had become 'tennis' in English.

Will

Nick and Terry!

You'll like this. I've found two surprise appearances of tennis in early English writing, both from around 1500! In 'The Second Shepherd's Play', a tennis ball is one of the gifts given by shepherds to the baby Jesus in Bethlehem, and in 'The Turke and Gawain', a story of King Arthur's round table, Sir Gawain plays tennis against 17 giants!

Mursili

THE ENGLISH KING HENRYS AND TENNIS By Al Hunter

Henry IV — HUGE tennis fan. 'Whether a chase is won or lost at tennis, Nobody can know until the ball is run': the earliest written appearance of the word 'tennis' in English. Found in a 1400 poem by John Gower dedicated to King Henry IV.

Henry V — Also a balls-out tennis fan. In Shakespeare's play 'Henry V', the French prince gives Henry a gift of tennis balls to suggest he is a frivolous youth and not to be taken seriously. The consequence? War, and the resounding defeat of the French at the Battle of Agincourt. The battle did happen in real life in 1415, but not because of a tennis-ball insult!

Henry VIII — Thought tennis was to die for. You couldn't keep him off the court. He was apparently playing tennis when he had his second wife, Anne Boleyn, arrested, and again when news arrived of her grisly end in the Tower of London.

WHAT, TENNIS?

'From pillar to post' means to be moved rapidly from one place to another, often in a disorientating way. But its link to tennis? It goes back to the original indoor version of the racquet-based game, now called 'real tennis' or 'royal tennis', which had pillars and posts on the court. A player skilfully running his or her opponent around was therefore sending them 'from pillar to post'.

Alan H (1980)

Great Innovations in Tennis
Part 1 — The Racquet By Lexi Hunter

For almost half the history of tennis, there was no racquet.
Mind-blowing! History shows us that the racquet probably came
along in the 16th century. The word comes from Middle French
'rachette' or 'requette'. But where did they come from? Maybe
from the Arabic word 'rahat', meaning palm of the hand. So, it
turns out 'racquet' is just another way of saying 'la paume'!

Tennis nearly had a very different name!
When Major Walter Clopton Wingfield decided to make
the break from royal tennis in 1873, he began patenting
box sets of racquets, balls, and nets for lawn play. But did
he call his semi-new game tennis? No. He called it
'sphairistike', from the Greek meaning skill at playing
at ball. He and his chums called it 'sticky' and played it
at garden parties. (As names go, it didn't stick!)
Fortunately, on his patent application, he added the
words 'or lawn tennis', and the rest is history.   Al

THE GAME OF
SPHAIRISTIKE
OR
LAWN TENNIS

W.C. WINGFIELD 1833~1912   1.50+50f
WIMBLEDON 1877

AVAILABLE AT ALL GOOD OUTDOOR SPORTS STORES

Seriously? Sphairistike? Sounds like
someone trying to describe toffee
while they're still chewing it ...   Lexi

Scoring in Tennis (because that needs explaining too)
By Al Hunter

The score that's most debated is 'love', the score you
have when you haven't scored at all. One theory says it
comes from the French 'l'oeuf' — 'the egg' — since an egg
looks like a zero. That might be convincing if the French
called it 'l'oeuf', but they just call it what it is —
'zero'.

So maybe 'love' is English. The expression 'to do
something for love', meaning to do it for nothing, dates
to the 1670s. 'Love' first appeared as a tennis score
about seventy years later, in 1742. Could it be that,
somewhere in between these times, to play for nothing, or
a score of nothing, came to be called 'playing for love'?

Once play starts, numbers come into it — 15, 30, 40. Why
them? And why not 45 to keep the pattern? It was
originally 15, 30, 45, from the clock, with 15 a quarter
of the way to winning the game, 30 halfway, and 45 three
quarters. But that was back when the scoring system was
French, and went 'quinze, trente, quarante-cinq'. 'Quinze,
trente, quarante' was thought to be more pleasing to the
ear, and the 'cinq' — the 5 on the end of the 45 — got
edited out before the score made its way into English.

If a game is tight, it can get to 40—40, and that has its
own name: deuce. French again, this time from 'a deux le
jeu', meaning to both is the game; that is, the scores
are equal.

Great Innovations in Tennis
Part 2 — The Lawn Mower By Lexi Hunter

Why is it so many modern sports have their origins in the mid-19th century? It's not like their ridiculous clothes were made for exercise! It's seriously possible that one big factor was the invention of the lawn mower in 1830. Once the grass could be sorted, it made sense to set land aside for games. As more people became interested in playing, official rules needed to be agreed on. Along came football codes, tennis, lawn bowls … you name it!

Patents and Inventions

Patent no 3642

What's wrong with a goat?

NOT APPROVED

Thank you

Goat Mower

A Timeline of Tennis Words by Alan Hunter

1510s — Court: came into English in the 12th century from Old French 'cort', meaning royal court or residence, but took more than three centuries to be applied to a place where tennis is played.

1600s — Fault: into English in the late 13th century as 'faute' meaning deficiency, or flaw, from Old French. Another word that took about three centuries to make its way into tennis.

It's rather more complicated than that. The Old French word came from the Latin 'falsus' meaning deceptive, but the subsequent use in tennis is closer to the early English meaning. The 'l' from the original Latin went back into 'faute' in the 16th century to create 'fault', but remained <u>not pronounced</u> until the 18th.

Montagu Hunter (1906)

1650s — Backhand: a word invented specifically for tennis. Not used figuratively, as in a 'backhanded compliment', until 1800.

Interesting gap here. It looks as if there are two notable eras of tennis language – one from the early game and another in the first decades of the modern game.   Mursili

1819 – *Volley:* came to English in the 1570s, meaning discharge of a number of guns at once, from Middle French 'volee' meaning flight. Borrowed by tennis to mean hitting the ball in mid-flight, before the bounce.

1879 – *Forehand:* originally an archery term, with 'forehand shaft' meaning an arrow for shooting directly in front (1540s).

Again, it's more complicated. The word evolved to mean position in front or above, and then prudent. 'Backhand' was created especially for tennis long after the invention of the word 'forehand', but 'forehand' wasn't actually used for the sport until 1879!

Montagu Hunter

1882 – *Smash:* meant a hard hit from 1725. From around 1700, it meant to kick downstairs. Came to describe the forceful overhead in tennis in 1882.

1898 – *Seed:* came into tennis as a verb by 1898, meaning to spread the better players evenly in the draw; became a noun referring to those players in 1924.

A Device for the Alteration of Space-Time

(to allow more efficient travel through both). Record made by my own hand, Caractacus, 480 AD

Nick and Terry,

See why this notebook needs to be kept in a vault with at least one python? If Caractacus's genius design for this time-travel peg were made public, chaos would most certainly ensue! Imagine if everyone started popping up throughout history like meerkats — it could rip apart the very fabric of space-time. Besides, while time travel may look like fun, the main equation you need to know is: (time travel) + (the Dark Ages) = (buckets of sick). So don't try this at home.

Yours in Words,
Mursili

- The travel matrix has some of the properties of a particle and some of a wave.

- Peg completes circuit, activates matrix.

- 'Feeling of pressure'? related to energy generated by travel in matrix with the contraction of space-time. $E^2 = p^2 v^2 + m^2 v^4$, but if mass of matrix is 0, $E = pv$. Unlikely to create a black hole (and destroy solar system) unless matrix has mass.

Thanks for not destroying the solar system. Next time perhaps let me put the theory to Mr Einstein before sending us out to put it into practice ...   Will H

Somebody buy that man a Large Hadron Collider.
Al

I agree. A collider's the perfect 21st-century gift for a mad 5th-century physicist who has everything ... but it's going in your backpack, not mine!
Lexi

Nick and Terry!

Your work as scribe and illuminator begins!

Lexi and Al Hunter have provided a timeline and are available for interview. Add your own research to this if you wish!

Do not rest until the story of the word 'busk' is told in its every detail. The smallest fact might be crucial to future hunters hunting this same word.

Yours in Words,
Mursili

WORD QUEST

Busk: to entertain [particularly to play music] in a public place, with the aim of receiving voluntary donations from passers by (from Fr [obsol] 'busquer', to steal, to prowl]

& MORE

1857 — 'busk' took on its modern meaning, to work as a roving entertainer

1851 — 'busk' meant to sell things in bars

1718 — 'busk' meant to cruise as a pirate

1590 — 'busquer' meant to steal or to prowl in French

1395 — 'busche' (or similar) meant bush in Middle French and 'buschers' beat the bushes to make birds take flight for hunting

Al

'THAT'S JUST SOME guy, playing covers and hoping you'll throw money into his guitar case,' Lexi said, as the word 'busk' glowed from the pages of the dictionary. 'It should say, "Alternative income source for musicians unable to get work in coffee shops."'

'Just wait.' Al moved closer, for a better look at the dictionary. 'The origins of plenty of words aren't as simple as they seem on the surface.'

He was pretty sure the past would throw up something other than just musicians hoping for coins.

He slipped his arms through the straps of his backpack. The weight of muesli bars and rope and all the gadgets took some effort to carry, but it was better than the alternative. At least this way they were ready for some things in the past, even if they couldn't be ready for everything. Soon pegs would appear in the backpack too, to lock the word down and carry them on to its source. He wondered where that might be, and who they might have to fight to get there.

'So,' Lexi said, 'are we doing this? Or are you just in a daze imagining the endless seventies classics that might be ahead of us? We should bring Dad along on this mission.'

Their father was such a fan of buskers he was too often inclined to join in. One time when he'd started singing, the busker had demanded more money.

'Imagine how gutted he'd be if we didn't save "busk",' Al said. 'We're doing it!'

Lexi tapped the '& more' button glowing from the dictionary. The room shuddered. The floor shook. They were falling on their way into the past again.

WORD
QUEST

They hit some small bumps, all in a rush, and then broke out from cloud above forested, snow-capped mountains. The cold air tore past their faces. They searched for cities, industries, straight lines cut for highways – any signs that they weren't too far back in time.

In the folds between the mountains, two creeks joined. Here buildings cropped up without much sense of order – a jumble of shingle roofs, smoke drifting from a few chimneys. A rough road leading out of town cut into the muddy landscape and followed the bends and bumps of the mountain.

Lexi and Al steered their fall to the edge of the forest and landed beside huge pine trees that looked like they had been there for centuries already.

They hid from view and Lexi reached into Al's bag. She pulled out five pegs, which meant this was the first of five time periods they would have to travel back to in order to save the word and keep it alive in the present.

Lexi held up the activated peg, the one with golden writing down its side. 'It says we're in "1857, Whiskeytown, California". Mean anything to you?'

Al checked his clothes. He was wearing patched overalls and a shirt that was missing a button-on collar. His boots went almost up to his knees, and his thighs were spattered with mud. He lifted the hat from his head. It was buckled and stained and had been in water more times than Mick Fanning.

'I think I'm a miner.' He turned to look at Lexi. She was dressed the same way. 'We're gold miners, and this is the California gold rush.'

'Okay.' Lexi straightened her hat, which Al thought looked even uglier than his. 'So, we've just got to find some poor guy who didn't cut it as a miner, and who's trying to make a buck out of music instead. Where do you think we should—'

Suddenly, there was a loud bang – a gunshot – and the sound of smashing glass.

'From what I've read,' Al said, 'the gold rushes weren't all about the music. I guess that tells us where we should be heading. Somewhere between us and the busker, this might be about to get interesting.'

'Really?' Lexi said. 'You're suggesting we go *towards* some guy who's shooting?'

'Or we could hide in the forest, miss the portal and have to work out how to live off the land before winter sets in.'

There was no choice, not really. Somewhere nearby, someone was about to say the word 'busk', perhaps for the very first time with its modern meaning. And a portal would open up that would take them further back into the past, so they could trace the word all the way back to its origins before returning home.

Among the scrappy buildings was probably a guy with a banjo or a washboard, desperate to make a buck. Maybe he was so awful someone was already shooting at him to make him stop.

'You go first,' Al said. 'They're a lot less likely to shoot a girl.'

'Oh, really?' Lexi put her hands on her muddy hips. 'You know that for a fact, history nerd? Well, I'm going first all right. But mainly because I've got more guts than some.'

She turned and started to stride towards the nearest building.

'Slowly,' Al said, in the loudest whisper he could manage,

before hurrying to catch up with her.

Together, they peered around the corner of the building. A wiry man in rough clothes much like there theirs stood in the middle of a cleared patch of dirt, facing a saloon and gripping a six-gun that looked too big for him to hold properly.

'You come out here now, Francis Creech!' he shouted. 'You come out here with every single ounce of my missing gold and no one 'cept you gets hurt!'

From behind a water barrel near the saloon's swinging doors, a hand reached out and carefully pulled a hat with some coins in it across the dirt.

Al watched in horror as the gunman lined his next shot up and fired, bringing up a spray of dirt next to the hat. There was a clatter and a clang as its owner flinched behind the barrel. His hand vanished.

'I don't got no gold,' he shouted out. 'I'm playin' for pennies. You know that.'

Nick,

That's all we've got? Maybe some of the kids we meet on school visits could get involved? No one would have to know. Just tell the kids what we've found out and let them write the rest of the story. What do you think?

Terry

Great — let's give them my notes.

Nick

Mix's Hotel
WHISKEYTOWN

What we've Found Out About the word 'Busk'

'Busk' didn't start out referring to that guy in the mall with his guitar case, or that girl with her violin, or the magician or mime further down the block.

The earliest clear modern use of 'busk' and 'busker' seems to date to 1857, during the California gold rush. Earlier that decade, a song wasn't all a busker might offer – by 1851 to busk was to sell in bars, whether you traded in goods (some of which might have been stolen...), bawdy ballads or stand-up comedy.

Before that, in the early 1700s, around the time Edward Teach became known as Blackbeard, to busk was to cruise as a pirate. The word moved into English from the French 'busquer', meaning to steal or prowl. But that's not the end of the trail.

'Busquer' probably comes from an earlier French word – perhaps 'busche' – meaning bush or firewood. And its connection with prowling? That might be the servants sent ahead to beat the bushes to flush out game for rich people to hunt. It's likely that those 'buschers', bent over and moving through the undergrowth, looking like prowlers, started it all centuries ago in France.

So, a lot of buskers' songs might only go for three minutes each, but the job title was hundreds of years in the making.

Nick

Found Letters

Twenty-three of the 26 letters of the English alphabet came from the Romans, but what about the others? All three are at risk of disappearing unless tracked to their origins and secured!

Caractacus

Step one? That has to be to track down the Latin alphabet. And here it is:

ABCDEFGHIKLM
NOPQRSTVXYZ

Notice what's missing? How could the Romans possibly go without J, U and W? Isn't the most famous Roman of all time a guy called Julius Caesar? How could half his first name not exist in his own time?

J

— Began as an 'I' written with a flourish, particularly if there were multiple 'I's (for example, xxiij became a stylish way to write xxiii, the Roman number 23).

— Some languages came to assign particular sounds to one letter or another, and the modern English 'J' sound came from French.

— In 1524, Italian poet and grammar nerd Gian Giorgio Trissino decided the alphabet needed to change to reflect the way people spoke, and recommended that when 'I' was a consonant it should be written as a 'J'.

Seems likely to have been a 'vocabolo cacciatore', a word hunter for the Italian language, who risked lifting the cloak of secrecy by tampering openly with the alphabet! Not recommended!

Mursili

U

- One of five letters descended from the Phoenician letter 'waw', which looked like a 'Y' but sounded more like a 'V' or a 'W'. So it's no surprise the five letters of ours it's related to are 'F', 'U', 'V', 'W' and 'Y'.

- Waw became the Greek letter 'upsilon', and the Romans took the small version of upsilon and wrote it as a 'V', using it for both the 'V' consonant sound and 'U' vowel sound. (Sounding strange? The English 'C' can make an 'S' or 'K' sound.)

- By the late Middle Ages, a round-bottomed version was introduced, with the pointed version ('V') used if it was at the beginning of a word and the rounded version ('U') used if it was in the middle or at the end. It was only the position which determined which one was used, not the sound.

- It was 1386 before the two versions appeared in an alphabet together.

- In the mid-16th century the pointed version became the consonant sound and the rounded version became the vowel sound.

W

- The history of 'U' explains why 'W' is written as double 'V' and yet called 'double U'.

- In Old English, the 'W' sound was made by the rune Þ ('wynn') but, with the arrival of the Normans, 'UU' and 'VV' started to be used.

- Wynn was gone by around 1300, and 'W' started to be treated as a letter, though it took another 200 years before it made it into the English alphabet.

- The Nordic countries took more convincing. 'W' officially made it into Norwegian in 1907, Danish in 1980 and Swedish in 2006. Finnish still treats it as a variant of 'V'.

I'm really not ready to start going through life as Terry VVhidborne, or Terry UUhidborne. Looks like I won't be going to Finland any time soon...

Doug!!!

Terry

All at Sea in Ancient Phoenicia

Nick and Terry,

Ah, the Phoenicians — great seafarers, even if we Hittites didn't always see eye-to-eye with them. You know Lebanon? Syria? Israel? The Phoenicians spread out from there across the Mediterranean, along with their famous purple dye and their alphabet. It was one of the earliest in existence, and the Greeks developed theirs from it around 800 BC, with the Romans developing the Latin alphabet from the Greek soon after.

YiW,
Mursili

It turns out the Phoenician alphabet isn't technically an alphabet at all — it's an abjad. An alphabet has vowels and consonants, while an abjad only has consonants. The Phoenician symbols that gave us our vowels originally made different sounds, for example, the letter ∃ ('he') was all about the 'h' part for Phoenicians, but the Greeks made it about the 'e' part. The Phoenician alphabet was a crucial step between Egyptian hieroglyphics and our alphabet, with each letter starting out as a picture of something, but coming to represent a sound. And here it is. ➞

Letter	Name	Meaning
∢	aleph	ox
◁	bet	house
⌐	gimel	camel
◁	dalet	door
∃	he	window
Y	waw	hook
I	zayin	weapon
日	heth	wall
⊗	teth	wheel
⊐	yodh	hand
⋊	kaph	palm (of a hand)
L	lamedh	goad
⑭	mem	water
५	nun	serpent, later whale
⧧	samekh	fish
O	ayin	eye
⊃	pe	mouth
⋎	tsade	hunt
ⵁ	qoph	needle head
⌐	resh	head
W	shin	tooth
X	taw	mark

In the library of Alexandria I found a document in Phoenician, which I have translated (with some difficulty, as Phoenician reads right-to-left) on the next page. It appears to be orders to a ship's captain, though the map with it is unclear. I have not yet been able to determine which route is the correct one. Hunters, please advise.

Nick and Terry,

Over to you. It is imperative we find out which colour route the captain took, or … I have no idea what might happen, to be honest. But the boss wants it, so thanks for taking it on without complaint.

YiW,
Mursili

GREEK	LATIN*
Aα	Aa
Bβ	Bb
ΓY	Cc, Gg
Δδ	Dd
Εε	Ee
(Ϝϝ), Yυ	Ff, Uu, Vv, Yy, Ww
Zζ	Zz
Hη	Hh
Θθ	–
Iι	Ii, Jj
Kκ	Kk
Λλ	Ll
Mμ	Mm
Nν	Nn
Ξξ poss. Xχ	poss Xx
Oo, Ωω	Oo
Ππ	Pp
(Mϻ)	–
(Ϙϙ), poss. Φφ, Ψψ	Qq
Pρ	Rr
Σoς	Ss
Tτ	Tt

*with modern additions

Seriously? My brain's too old for this. Terry - this is one for those school kids you were talking about. Any decent book with a puzzle like this would have the answer on the last page...

Nick

Sail from Byblos with eight bundles of best papyrus, two jars of Tyrian purple dye and two jars of indigo. Plot a course to Ibiza, where you will deliver two bundles of papyrus and pick up six jars of fish sauce. Proceed to Carthage where you will deliver to Queen Dido all four jars of dye and six bundles of papyrus. From the Queen, take four chests of gold and deliver to her brother, King Pygmalion of Tyre, by the most direct route. Collect six jars of Tyrian purple dye and return to Byblos.

But Nick, puzzles are awesome! I've already started figuring out some of the translations. Remember that Phoenician is written right-to-left and they didn't write vowels, unless they were making a non-vowel sound (thanks for the tip, Lexi).

Terry

Recent name	Phoenician name	Partial translation	Full translation
Byblos	TZOR	MSKI	xwⵣ⵿◻×9Φ
Sidon	LPQY	SND	∟🇾1
Carthage	GEBAL	RDGA	ⵞywⵏꙴ
Tyre	IBOSIM	TSDH TRQ	ꙴ◁ꓘ
Leptis Magna	IKSM	LBG	yywꓘ
Algiers	TZIDHON	RY	ꓭ◁1ꓚ
Ibiza	AGADIR	MSBI	�◻ꓘ
Cadiz	QART HADAST	YQPL	ꓹꓻꓭ

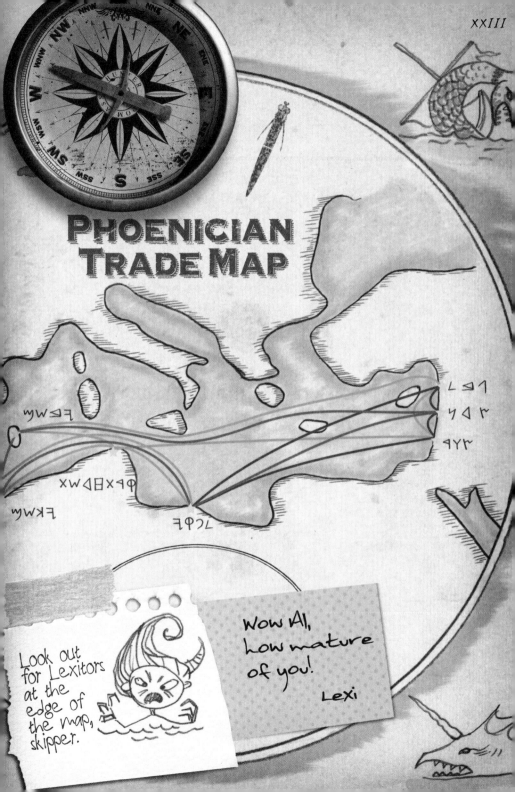

Hittite Bread #181
By Mursili

Caractacus, you would be amazed how easy it is to make ninda in the 21st century (or, as you call it, bread or hlaf). You can buy the grains already milled to tiny, tiny specks!

That'd be called a 'loaf' anytime in the last 700 years, Mursili, in case you were wondering.
Al

We Hittites love bread. I could be so bold as to say we were the first people to bring it to perfection, in any one of the 180 different official ways to make it. Under the laws of King Suppi, many breads are purely for the gods, some are for King Suppi and some for making beer. But here is one glorious ninda where there are no penalties for making it only to eat! I know this because it is my mother's own recipe. All ingredients are local to Hattusa. Well, other than that tiny bit of salt from King Suppi's salt mines. And rolling the breads in sesame seeds can even help appease the Storm God! That perhaps only applies if you place the breads in the house of the Storm God. However, if the weather is not threatening, I say eat them!

1 cup of red lentils

4 cups of wholemeal flour, plus more for kneading

1/2 cup of olive oil

2 handfuls of olives, seeds removed, chopped

1/2 teaspoon of salt

sesame seeds

This means you too, Lexi :) Al

Remove all livestock and other animals from the kitchen. Cut your beard and hair short or contain them effectively. This is the law!

←

Boil two cups of water, add lentils and simmer until the water is absorbed (about ten minutes). Allow lentils to cool.

Mix flour, two cups of water, olive oil and salt. Mix in the cooked lentils and olives. Knead, then break into pieces and form into flat, round patties. Cover both sides of patties with sesame seeds. Cover with a tea towel and leave overnight.

Next day, ~~make a fire from best quality dried dung (sheep or goat)~~, with the help of a responsible, clean-shaven adult, heat an oven to 180°C (160°C fan-forced) and bake for 40 minutes.

Goes nicely with cheese and fig paste or dips like hommus or babaganoush.

Lexi

Lost Letters — Will Hunter

Yes, some letters were found to add to the 23 of the Roman alphabet, but not just 'J', 'U' and 'W'. There were at least nine more: If they had all stayed, the alphabet would now be 35 letters long! At Caractacus's request, Will has attempted to find out when and why they went missing.

The Runes

Ƿ ƿ (wynn)

- A rune letter that replaced 'uu/vv' and worked as a 'w'.

- Lasted until around 1300, when 'uu/vv' took over again, probably influenced by the French, through the deliberate actions of Norman scribes seeking to eliminate non-Roman letters.

Þ þ (thorn)

- A rune letter that made a 'th' sound.

- In regular use until 1500 and used in the King James Bible (1611).

- Could be said to be the last rune in use in English. When William Caxton printed the first book in English, he used German type, which had no thorn. So he used a capital 'Y', making 'the' appear as 'Ye', something still occasionally seen in signs like 'Ye Olde Curiosity Shoppe' and almost always mispronounced.

I don't know why you didn't keep this one. Much more sensible than writing that sound as a 't' followed by an 'h'. — Caractacus

The Borrowings

Ʒ ʒ (yogh)

- Some of the missionaries who arrived in England in the 7th century to convert the locals to Christianity were Irish. They brought their 'g' with them and it became part of Old English.

- When Middle English brought 'g' back from French, some people kept using 'ʒ' as well, so it needed its own name. By then, 'ʒ' made a range of sounds, including a 'g' sound, a 'y' sound and the 'ch' sound we now think of as Scottish. For example, 'niʒt', meaning the opposite of day, was pronounced as 'nicht'.

- Norman scribes, in their purge of non-Roman letters, replaced 'ʒ' with 'gh'. Because 'ʒ' made a range of sounds, this explains a lot of odd 'gh's now in English words. 'Niʒt', pronounced 'nicht', became written as 'night', and eventually the way we said it changed too.

- It took until the late 15th century before the work of the Normans (and their successors) was complete, and 'ʒ' was gone.

Ð ð (eth)

- An Irish letter originating as a crossed 'D' and making the same 'th' sound as the rune 'Þ' (thorn) in Old English.

- Possibly first used in English to make the unvoiced 'th' (as in 'think') with 'Þ' used for the voiced (as in 'this'), but any distinction was quickly lost, making two symbols unnecessary.

- Gone from English by 1300, but survives in Icelandic.

ſ (long 's')

- Developed from the 's' in the Old Roman cursive (everyday Roman handwriting around 2000 years ago).

- Became more vertical towards the end of the 8th century as upper and lowercase letters developed.

- Used as an 's' at the beginning or in the middle of words, but almost never at the end, and also used as the first 's' of any double 's'.

- Looked dangerously like an 'f' and wasn't really necessary, so printers started giving it up in the late 18th century, with John Bell of the British Letter Foundry leading the way.

- From 10 September 1803, 'The Times' used only the short 's'.

⁊ (ond)

- Roman scribe Marcus Tullius Tiro's shorthand for 'and' more than 2000 years ago.

- Tiro's system had 4000 signs, but this grew to 13,000 by the Middle Ages.

- Writing in code drew suspicion for being involved in witchcraft and magic, so Tironian notes were gone by the 17th century, with '⁊' surviving in Gaelic representing 'and'. It is still seen on Irish road signs today.

-Will

The Ligatures

Ligatures are two letters tied together. For example, 'w' started out as a ligature – 'uu' or 'vv' joined together.

& (ampersand)

– Began around 2000 years ago as a ligature of 'et', the Latin word for 'and', and evolved over centuries to look the way it now does.

– Long regarded as the final letter of the alphabet, so that, once 'j', 'u' and 'w' were included, the alphabet was commonly considered 27 letters long, as late as the 19th century.

– '&' gets its name from the alphabet being recited at schools and finishing with 'and "and" by itself', but this was said in Latin: 'and per se and'. And exactly how clear is a classroom of school students at reciting things? Not very. So, 'and per se and' slurred into 'ampersand', and the word was commonly in use by 1837.

Æ æ (ash)

– A Latin ligature (in this case joining 'a' and 'e' together) later given the name of a rune.

– Used until the 20th century for words like 'encyclopædia' and 'mediæval' but by then not considered a letter (more recently replaced by either 'ae' or just 'e').

– Still in use in Scandinavian alphabets.

Œ œ (ethel)

– Another Latin ligature (joining 'o' and 'e') later given the name of a rune.

– Used until the 20th century for words like 'diarrhœa' and 'phœnix' but by then not considered a letter (more recently replaced by either 'oe' or just 'e').

– Still used in French, with 'œ' and 'oe' pronounced differently.

WORD QUEST Feisty.

spirited, aggressive, touchy.

Typically applied to a person who is relatively small [American English, from 'feist', small dog]

& MORE

1896
'feisty' – aggressive, touchy, spirited

1770
'feist', 'foist', 'fist' or 'fice' – a small crossbred hunting dog

1520s
'fysting curre' – stinking mongrel dog

500BC (approx)
'fistiz' – fart (PGMc)

3500BC (very approx)
'pezd' – fart (PIE)

'**I**'M SURPRISED THERE'S not a picture of you,' Al said to Lexi when he saw the word 'feisty' glowing on the page.

'There are worse things to be than feisty.' Lexi snatched the dictionary from him and checked the definition. 'Small dog. I bet it doesn't mean a friendly small dog.'

Already she was imagining dog bites, rabies. Her version of the first appearance of feisty was happening in a dirty alley, the mutt growling and frothing, in some horrible, stinky century she'd prefer not to visit again.

'Oh, come on,' Al said. 'It says it's a small dog. It's not the Battle of Hastings.'

'I was nearly killed at the Battle of Hastings.'

'But you weren't. See my point? Ten thousand heavily armed Norman soldiers versus … a small dog.'

She read the definition again. There was no hint of anything worse, not that that was something to be confident about. But Al was all set to go, his backpack already slung over his shoulders.

'Fine, but if we come across any dogs, I'm using you as my human shield,' she said, reaching for the glowing '& more' button.

The floor swayed and the windows rattled. The rug beneath their feet started to drift up and down, and then dropped away. And they fell.

They braced for bumps, but the bumps were over almost as soon as they'd begun, and Lexi and Al slipped from damp low clouds to an overcast afternoon. Al could just make out the grey water of the sea on one side of a peninsula and a bay on the other, before city streets, the roofs of houses, then trams and carriages came into view. He guessed it might be 1870 to 1910. Earlier and there would have been no trams, later and there would have been cars.

All of a sudden he was aware of a weight in his hand. It was a bucket of oranges. What could a bucket of oranges have to do with feistiness, or small dogs for that matter?

Lexi hit the ground in a billow of bloomers and flaps of navy fabric. The clothes caught her legs and she tumbled onto the edge of the street outside a large brick building.

As she stood up and beat the dust from her cape, Al said, 'I thought you were a bag of laundry for a second there.'

Lexi straightened her shoulders and glared at him. Her braided hair was tied up with blue ribbon. Her cape, with its huge collar, was buttoned at the neck. Her bloomers puffed out to below her knees, where they were tucked into black boots. Only her head and hands weren't covered by some item of clothing.

'Knickerbockers,' she said, pointing to Al's baggy brown below-the-knee pants where they met his toffee-coloured socks. The ensemble made his calves look even scrawnier than usual. 'Orange boy, I don't think either of us wins the wardrobe comp this time.'

Lexi stepped behind him and reached into his canvas knapsack.

'Five pegs,' she said, as she pulled out the activated one. It read '1896, San Francisco, California'. She passed the peg to Al and said, 'Tell me nothing too awful's about to happen.'

Al glanced up and down the street. In both directions, trams were moving away from them. A family passed by in

AIRSHIP California Orange

an open carriage. All he could see was people getting on with their day.

'I've got nothing,' he told her. 'It's not a big gold-rush time, the earthquake's not for another ten years ...'

Just then, the double timber doors of the large brick building opened.

'My, you Berkeley girls have lovely hair,' a woman said.

She stood, framed by the doorway, wearing a dark skirt and jacket. She made a note of something on a leather-backed pad before tucking her pencil into its holder and extending her hand.

'Mabel Craft. I'm covering this for the *Chronicle.*'

'Lexi Hunter.' She held out her hand. It was clear Mabel Craft had been talking only to her. But who was Mabel Craft? And was the *Chronicle* a newspaper? What was about to happen that a newspaper reporter would come to see? 'I didn't realise the *Chronicle* would be here.'

'You're about to make history. Can't miss that,' Mabel said. 'You should come inside. The rest of your team's here already.'

As Lexi and Al stepped towards the doorway, still not sure what history they – or at least Lexi – might be about to make, a woman in black appeared beside Mabel and thrust the point of a stick in Al's direction.

'No men in here,' she said sternly. 'Not today. Everyone knows that. Even little men.'

Lexi held back a laugh. The woman reached the tip of her stick to Al's chest and nudged him with it.

'Oh, Mrs Magee,' Mabel said calmly. 'Look, he's your team's orange boy. You have to let him in or they'll have no nourishment at half-time. They'll collapse in the second half and it'll be called a Stanford plot.'

Mrs Magee lowered the tip of her stick.

'Very well,' she said, still sternly, to Al. 'But you are to wait in a side room and cut your oranges there. You are not to speak, or to alert the ladies to your male presence. If women's basketball is to go beyond this first college game, it will be because we avoided turning it into a spectacle for men.'

She stepped inside and pulled the door fully open.

As they followed her, Lexi nudged Al and pointed to Mrs Magee's back. 'Feisty?'

'She's not feisty,' Al said. 'She's just rude. I'm sticking with the reporter. I bet it's going to come from her. Or maybe it'll be up to you to get out on the court and be feisty?'

Terry,
Look at the heap of work that librarian's dumped on us ... where are those kids you talked about? Let's get them to finish this story.
Nick

What We've Found Out About the Word 'Feisty'

'Feisty' is quite a recent word, with ancient origins that might surprise you. Its current meaning, referring to someone who is forceful or spirited, often in the face of challenging opposition (and often a short person), dates back to America in the 1890s.

A 'feist' (or 'foist', 'fist' or 'fice') was typically a small crossbred dog that would rush to take on a bigger opponent. The earliest written reference comes from George Washington, long before he became US president, when he was a wealthy plantation owner in Virginia. In 1770, his diary records his concerns about his dog Countess, a frequent escaper from the kennel, who had mated twice with 'a small foist looking yellow cur' (a 'cur' being an undesirable dog).

But where does 'feist' and its variants as a name for dogs come from? It's a contraction of 'fysting curre', first recorded in English in the 1520s and meaning a stinking mongrel dog. Literally stinking – the 'fysting' part comes from the Middle English word 'fysten', meaning to fart!

Tracking further back beyond written records to reconstructed languages, 'fysten' probably came from a Proto-Germanic word like 'fistiz'. Proto-Germanic, the basis for many modern European languages, was spoken for about a thousand years from around 500BC in the regions we now know as southern Scandinavia and northern Germany.

But since the fart itself long pre-dates any language to describe it, it makes sense to take a step further back, to as far as we can go, to the origins of the Proto-Indo-European language near the Black Sea more than 5000 years ago. It's likely there were at least two words for fart: 'perd' (not far from 'fart', really) and 'pezd', which might well be the origin of 'fistiz'.

Nick

A HITTITE TRIES TO GET HIS HEAD AROUND THE POPULAR GAME OF

~~KRIK KET~~ ~~CRECKETT~~

CRICKET

Nick and Terry,
A game that involves a duck, a trick with a hat and whatever on earth a googly is? I had to try to get to the bottom of it And maybe the top too.

YiW,
Mursili

Look! Here's the first ever reference to cricket in English!

'Being a scholler in the ffree schoole of Guldeford, hee and diverse of his fellows did runne and play there at creckett and other plaies.'

The coroner John Derrick recalling his 1550s childhood in court documents in 1598.

Nuns and monks play cricket in the 14th century

I have examined this 'creckett' further and determined it came from the French word 'criquet', meaning a goal post or stick. This probably came from the earlier Dutch or Flemish word 'cricke', meaning a stick or staff. Which means we should be calling the bat the cricket instead!

BASIC CRICKET WORDS by Mursili

Bat: In Old English, 'batt' meant a club or cudgel (a word now sadly underused). Early cricket bats were shaped more like clubs (fatter at the bottom end), since most bowling was delivered fast underarm.

Wicket: By the early 13th century, a small door or gate was known as a 'wicket' (from Old Northern French). By about 1733, it came to be used for the arrangement of stumps in cricket, possibly because early versions of the game had used wickets of the small-gate variety from sheep pens. 'To take a wicket' means to get a batter out.

Bail: I have learned that the wicket is made up of the stumps (the tall straight sticks) and the bails (the short knobbly sticks on top that fall off when the wicket is hit). But the association of the word 'bail' with 'wicket' goes back long before cricket. Centuries ago, 'bail' was used in a number of ways referring to fences, and one kind of bail probably latched the sheep wicket at the top.

Stump: If you couldn't find a sheep wicket in the early days of the game, you might've had to make do with a tree stump. But the lack of bails on top caused a lot of arguments about dismissals, so the wicket was preferred, and the individual sticks became known as stumps.

Crease: 'Crease' came from 'creaste', a variant of 'crest', meaning ridge. It first appeared in the 1660s and referred to a fold in a cloth (which, I believe, it still does). By 1779, it had been claimed by cricket, though the crease was then cut in the ground. The crease only became a white line in the late 19th century.

Some think the early cricket ball was made from a ball of wool.

Al

1770   2016

Bails
Motion sensors
Flashing LED lights

22.5cm

70cm

Camera
Microphone

Ground

Data transmitter

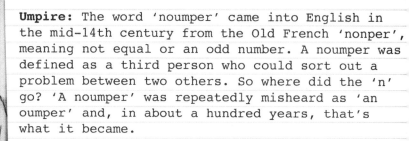

Umpire: The word 'noumper' came into English in the mid-14th century from the Old French 'nonper', meaning not equal or an odd number. A noumper was defined as a third person who could sort out a problem between two others. So where did the 'n' go? 'A noumper' was repeatedly misheard as 'an oumper' and, in about a hundred years, that's what it became.

Odd Cricket Words by Lexi Hunter

Okay, Mursili, as you've probably noticed, there's way more to cricket words than just what the bits and pieces are called. So, I thought I'd help you out with some of my favourites:

Maiden — Well, there was this knight in shining armour and a dragon and a … no, it's not that dramatic! Each over (made up of six deliveries by the bowler) gets its own little box on the scoresheet where the scorer writes the number of runs from each ball. No score from any balls that over equals an untouched scoresheet, which to someone (I suspect someone creepy!) seemed as pure as a young girl, hence the name maiden.

Duck — Apparently, a duck's egg looks like a zero.

As opposed to other eggs? Ever seen an egg that looked like, say, a seven? I didn't think so.   Al

When a batsman ended up with zero as his score, they called it a 'duck's egg'. Which I would have shortened to 'egg', since it's the zero-shaped bit, but no, those crazy old cricket guys shortened it to the word meaning a webbed-footed water fowl.

Hat-trick — I can see how a bowler getting three wickets with three consecutive balls is a cool trick, but what does it have to do with hats? Well, a long, long time ago, when a bowler pulled off this feat, he got to claim a new hat from his club, or got to pass his old one around for cash.

French cut — Invented by the French? No. This dodgy accidental shot is also known as a Chinese cut, a Staffordshire cut, a Surrey cut, etc. Basically you name it after someplace you want to be mean about, and it becomes your in-joke about how people from there are hopeless at cricket. My new name for it? The 'Al cut'.

Googly — A googly is a tricky piece of bowling that looks like leg spin but turns like off spin. Maybe it was called that as it's so cunning it makes your eyes go googly. No one's sure. We do know that 'googly' and 'eyes' go together as far back as 1901, and the first reference to the googly in cricket comes from just two years later. Well, apparently. No one can find it. But the English captain of the time, Pelham Warner, swore he read it then in a newspaper on a tour of New Zealand.

Oh, and one other thing. It's not a word, but it's a fact worth knowing. Those dresses I always seem to end up wearing when we plunge into the past? The ones that have about fifty skirts and make me look like a nanna's frilly toilet-roll cover? Apparently, they might have done one good thing for the sport of cricket. Bowling was strictly underarm until, just over two hundred years ago, Christina Willes was playing with her brother John, but couldn't bowl the way she was supposed to because of all those skirts. So, she bowled sidearm instead. John took the action into first-class cricket and bowling arms got higher and higher until overarm bowling was finally legalised in 1864.

Nick and Terry! I've hidden more information about cricket terms on a marvellous thing called the internet. Go to **wordhunters.com.au** to investigate!

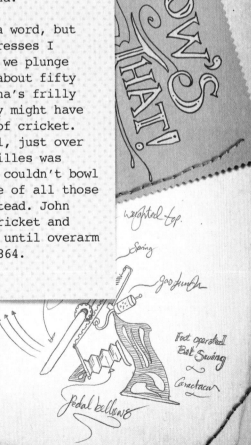

weighted top.

Spring

gas jundon

Foot operated Bat Sewing

Caractacus

pedal bellows

HAT TRICK CRICKET

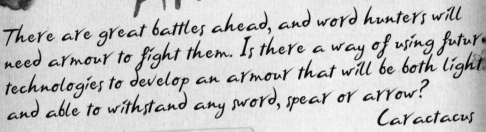

Fyrdraca scealu heaðureaf
Dragon Scale Armour

There are great battles ahead, and word hunters will need armour to fight them. Is there a way of using future technologies to develop an armour that will be both light and able to withstand any sword, spear or arrow?

Caractacus

Dear Alan,
Thank you for your advice that ceramic armour is stronger than iron, as well as being much lighter. If only you could fit a ceramic manufactory in one of your packs. It's rather challenging to make armour-grade ceramic tiles in the 490s! I suppose it's no surprise since phosphorous, one of the main ingredients, wasn't discovered until 1669!

Caractacus

Dear Caractacus,
My research tells me that there are two resources plentiful in your time which can provide the element you need (phosphorus). One is huge amounts of stale urine, the other is bones. The steps you need to take are listed next, and I assume you have chosen to use bones.
Alan

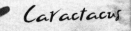

1. Make phosphorus

- Burn bones to a fine powder in lime kiln.
- Place powder in a tub with equal amounts of boiling water and oil of vitriol (oil of vitriol = sulphuric acid).

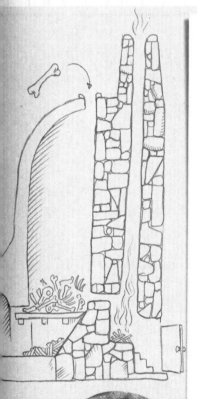

- Keep warm and stir occasionally for 21 hours. Allow to rest and cool for a further 12 hours.
- Decant liquid, run through a fine filter, allow to settle and decant again.
- Over heat, evaporate until mixture is a syrupy consistency.
- Add finely powdered charcoal (one part charcoal to five parts syrup) to decompose residual oil of vitriol (requires good ventilation – far from easily achieved in a 490s house, I realise ...)
- Heat to burn charcoal, producing elemental phosphorous.

The carbon from the charcoal strips oxygen from the phosphoric acid, leaving elemental phosphorous.

2. Convert phosphorous into a polymer

- Burn phosphorous to produce phosphorous pentoxide.
- Add one measure of water to ten measures phosphorous pentoxide, causing the phosphorous pentoxide molecules to join up, forming polymers.
- Skim polymers and spin to separate.
- Remove innermost layer (molecules all too small and not useful) and discard.
- Remaining material to be used in sintering (see below).

$$P_4 + 5O_2 \rightarrow P_4O_{10}$$

← Glue

3. Create binder

- Boil hooves and bones.
- Skim surface fat and allow to cool until gelatinous in texture.

4. Sintering

- Mix five parts quartz powder with one part phosphate polymer and add enough water and binder to create a slurry. ←

Consistency of a thick liquid or sloppy paste

- Spray-dry slurry into a powder.
- Press powder into plate moulds.
- Heat to burn off the binder.
- Increase heat to make powder particles and then fuse into ceramic plates.

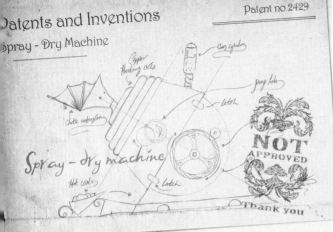

Patents and Inventions

Patent no 2429

Spray - Dry Machine

Copper Heating coils

Gas cylinder

peep hole

Late extrusion

latch

NOT APPROVED

Spray - dry machine

Hot coolers

latch

Thank you

Finally! I've spent most of the fifth century getting through steps one to four ...

5. Make garment
- Prepare fabric backing.
- Sew plates into place, with attachment points covered by plates above.
- Attach fabric outer layer.

Scale armour first seen among the Scythians (witnessed while hunting 'toxic'), and then, it appears, improved upon by the Romans. Your King Vortigern would have done well to maintain such Roman practices.

Timeline of 'Toxic'
1664 in English
1212 in Old French as 'toxique'
890 in Medieval Latin as 'toxicus' meaning poisoned
220BC in Latin as 'toxicum' meaning poison
339BC in Greek as 'toxikon pharmakon' meaning poison for arrows, from 'toxon' meaning bow
580BC in Scythian as 'takhsha' meaning bow, or branch of a yew tree

Note to future hunters: 339BC is the risky one here – the Scythian king, Ateas, might have been ninety, but he wasn't one to back away from a fight. The decisive battle in his conflict with the Macedonians occurred near the Danube estuary, and ended with Macedonian victory.

Montagu Hunter

MAKE YOUR OWN ARMOUR!

Nick and Terry,
Here is something we do in the library at Cubberla Creek State School when we feel like 'getting medieval'! We make cardboard suits of armour and then have sword fights with cardboard tubes. Note: the presence of a helmet does not excuse blows to the head! There are eyes up there, so keep your tube sword low and play nice. Here are the pieces you need for a full suit of armour, 1420s-style. Suit up!

Yours in Words (and Cardboard Armour),
Mursili

Optional holes

GREAT HELM: This is the easiest helmet to make, since it is just a cylinder on your head. Measure the circumference of your head, and cut a rectangle with this measurement as the length of one side and the approximate height you want as the other. Ask your valet to wrap it around your head, with the join at the back, to work out where eye and nose holes need to go. Cut eye holes and make a flap for the nose. Fasten the edges at the back.

GORGET: This goes around the neck, so cut a strip of cardboard long enough to do that, and make it wider in the middle than at the ends, since more protection is needed at the front.

PAULDRONS (two): These cover your shoulders. Cut two teardrop-shaped pieces of cardboard 20-25cm long, then cut out a segment from the fat end of teardrop. Join the two edges of the gap you've made. Your pauldrons should now cup your shoulders.

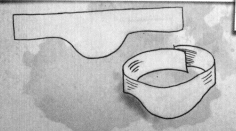

BASEGAWS (two): Armpit armour! Because who wants to get jabbed in the armpit? Ouch! Cut two circles of cardboard about 10cm in diameter, and attach one to the front lower edge of each of your pauldrons. For extra armpit security, also attach to the cuirass (next page).

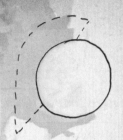

COUTER (two): Elbow protection. Make two cardboard tubes that fit very loosely around your elbows and are about 15cm in height. While each is still a rectangle (before you make it permanently into a tube), cut a triangle from the middle of either end. This triangle should have a base of no more than 5cm, and go about halfway to the middle of the piece of cardboard. Now join the cut edges to form a tube. You will see there is a 'wedge' missing. Close it up to create your elbow joint.

VAMBRACE (two): The vambrace can be a simple cylinder of cardboard protecting your forearm, or you can build in hand protection by making a longer tube and cutting a piece out of one end, as shown. The bit that sticks out protects the back of your hand.

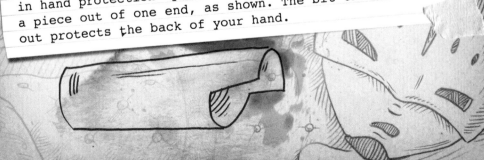

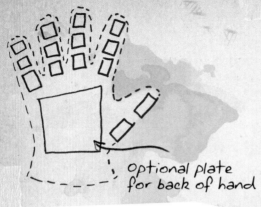

Optional plate
for back of hand

GAUNTLETS (two): Take a pair of washing-up or gardening gloves. Chop offcuts of your cardboard into small rectangles, three for each finger and two for each thumb (to match the bones in your hand). Tape them to the fingers and thumbs of the gloves.

CUIRASS: Now for the big one — body protection. To cover your chest and back, measure from the top of your pants at the front, up your torso, over your shoulders and down your back to the top of your pants again. You need a piece of cardboard that length. For the width, measure the front half of your chest. Next you need to cut out a head hole and room for your shoulders, as shown. Decorate the front with a fancy crest or coat of arms. To wear this armour, place it over your head and join at the sides.

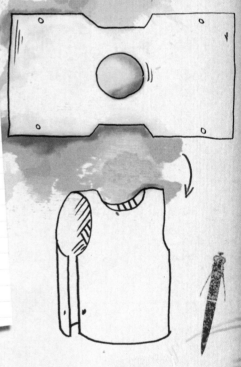

FAULDS (two): Rectangular pieces of cardboard curved to cover the hips, attached to the bottom of the cuirass, and to each other in the middle.

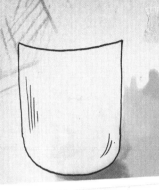

TASSETS (two): Longer rectangular pieces of cardboard, also curved, in this case to cover the thighs. Attach to the bottom of the cuirass or faulds, whichever feels more comfortable.

CUISSES AND POLEYNS (two): Your lower thighs and knees need protection too, in case someone lying on the ground tries to stab you (with their cardboard tube, I mean). The cuisses protect the thigh and the poleyns protect the knee, but it's quite okay to combine them, couter-style.

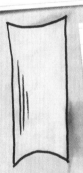

GREAVES (two): Shin protection. Two options here. You can either focus on the shin bone (covering each one with a curved rectangle of cardboard and holding it in place with elastic around the calf muscle) or you can cover the whole lower leg (another cardboard tube).

SABATONS (two): Okay, so you could add a pair of sabatons (foot armour), but feet only ever got attacked when a knight was on horseback. So, unless you're riding into battle, you can do without sabatons. In fact, knights fighting on foot usually did, since sabatons were hard to move in, particularly if the ground was wet or muddy.

And you're done. Now imagine it weighs 25kg and try fighting in that!

A Chronicle OF THE HUNTERS (Incomplete)

Name	Background
ᚠᛚᛏᚠ ᚾᛆᛏᛏᚠ (500-?512)	Hunter and woodland dweller near Northwic, East Angle Lands
Æthelberht, hunta (?512 - 536)	Hunter and mystic, outside Westwic, East Angle Lands
Wulfar, hunta (536 - ?)	Hunter and poacher, Cratendune, Lands of the South Gyrwas
Tonberht, hunta (547 - 562)	Hunter and exiled prince of the North Gyrwas, Cratendune, Lands of the South Gyrwas
Cynewulf, hunta (667-689)	Hunter, poet and monk, Medeshamstede, Mercia
Cynegurga, huntester (689-702)	Hunter, outlaw, practitioner of old magic, Medeshamstede, Mercia

Nick and Terry,
The number listed is a measure of how many words need saving. Sometimes the dictionary is very stable (a score of 10, or close to it), with very few words activating and requiring hunting to continue existing. At other times, many words become unstable and activate, leading to a lower score. Some word hunters work very hard for the money*. Be assured Caractacus is constantly working to improve the stability of the dictionary, while at the same time keeping it flexible enough to take in new words.

YiW,
Mursili
*There is no money.

Dictionary Stability	Hunted	Notes
9	rade Þeod	1: Not a reader, but had a good ear and could move with speed through forest.
		2: Dictionary stable from 508 to 522. In possession of Æthelberht, son of Octa from around 512
9	hÞæt swutelað fleot	Too interested in 'magic' for my liking and turning it to his own use.
9	Þæt wicca	Lost while hunting 'wicca'. Dictionary subsequently found in hunter's hide by Tonberht.
8	grindan folc hælp genog he sceaga	An effective hunter, but always searching for 'spells' that would help him overthrow Eorcenberht the Usurper.
10	no hunts conducted	We only found out about him later, when the following hunter found his name written in the dictionary, in the Irish hand, in charcoal. Only the third hunter with some capacity to read and write. Shame more use was not made of him.
9	oxen Wyrcan	She gave me some good pointers on leaves, bark and so on as medicines, poisons and for managing stubborn stains!
7		

Name	Background	Dictionary Stability
Wulfstan, hunte (1112 – 1135)	Hunter, skinner, leather worker, Oswaldslow, Worcestershire	9
Mathilde Hunte (1135 – ?1141)	Daughter of Wulfstan, nun, Worcester	9
Ranulfe Hunte (?1141 – 1152)	Falconer, Worcester	8
Peter Hunter (1358 – 1368)	Collector of taxes on moveables, Bristol	8
Henry Hunter (1368 – ?1380)	Clerk to the Bishop of Bath and Wells, Wells, Somerset	8
Edward Hunter (?1380 – ?1390)	Schoolteacher, Wells, Somerset	8

HUNTERS

Hunted	Notes
fleon ordel	Lost hunting 'ordel'. Ordel consequently lost from English and re-entered as 'ordeal' from Middle French in the mid-16th century.
blæco	Took the job very seriously. Blamed me for her father going missing. We also lost a perfectly good word for about 450 years!
tigele fixen pencan plega	Travelled with falcons, which seemed to get him out of some difficult situations. Should recommend to other hunters. Very concerned with the way his hair was tossed by travel.

harrow fower measles grim	Suspicious by nature, but a sound solver of problems.
snot, slore, swivel, lack	Kept complaining he deserved 'better words'.
nest, evil	Not at all happy with the Old English approach to spelling. Presumed lost hunting 'evil' around 1390. Dictionary not located until 1406. No record of words lost during that time.

Lemuel Hunter (1594 - 1596)	Scrounger (thank you, Will Hunter, for that very useful word from 1915), formerly taverner at the Duck and Drake, London	6
John Hunter (1596 - ?)	In service to a Viscount, mercenary in Spain (possibly for Spain), resident London and elsewhere	2
Montagu Hunter, CB (1906 - ?)	Assistant Under-Secretary of State for the Colonies, London	4
Emmeline Hunter (1909 - 1915)	Poor Law guardian, local organiser, Women's Social and Political Union, London	5
Agnes Hunter (1915 - ?)	Scholarship student, St Paul's Girls' School, London	3
Will Hunter (1918) (2012 - 13)	Apprentice carpenter, London	2

halloo, race, twill, grind, quint

Not one for a complicated task. Unusually short period as dictionary custodian. Missing? Tenure interrupted?

drudge, fordo, batten, shaw, afeared, fever, island, barn

Inquisitive. Needs watching...

rather, stour, fortune, grace, toxic, read

Set in his ways, but competent. Missing from late 1906 or early 1907. Last seen with 'redan' in Northwic while hunting 'read'. Was he compromised further back on this hunt or early on the next?

water, idle, cloud, teasel, yoghurt, kiosk, hair, choice, shape, tawdry, hurt

Reports she found dictionary with a bookmark in it at the page 'guitar' to 'gyrate', with a mark next to 'guy'. Could Montagu have been hunting 'guy' when he disappeared?

haunt, danger, hint, lord, good, blatant

Her mark has been found in the 1650s, when the word 'blatant' came into general use, but not in 1596, when Spenser coined it for The Faerie Queen. Lost in London in 1596? Other hunters have been requested to seek her near the lodgings and bookshop of Spenser's publisher, William Ponsonby.

roke, OK, toxin, gun, thing, cocoa, bolt, hustings, hello, dollar, gun, ye, tawdry, weird

Dictionary stability too low to allow complete list of words hunted. Resourceful hunter. Lost while hunting 'hello'.

Found by future hunters in 1839. Restored to hunter status. Fought in the Battle of Grendlaw before returning to his own time.

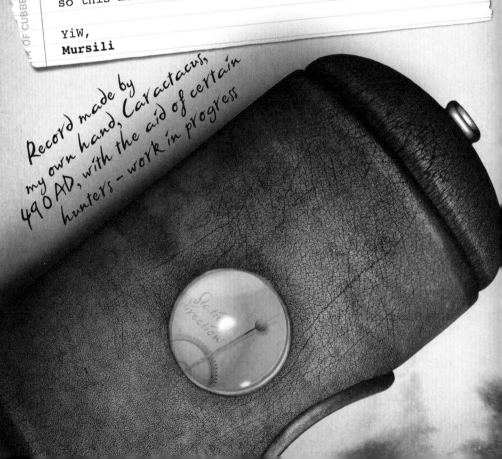

An Aid to Portal Location
(Olfactory/Electrostatic)

Nick and Terry,

You know where the top secrets go? Place this one on top of that. The portals are the way we word hunters travel from one era to another. They open up the instant a word evolves, and we lock the word in place and leap through the portal to keep travelling. Control of the portals means control of the language, so this must not fall into the wrong hands!

YiW,
Mursili

Record made by
my own hand, Caractacus,
490 AD, with the aid of certain
hunters – work in progress

Skate Direction

While the odds of prompt portal location can be greatly enhanced by correct travel techniques, it is understood that the search can at times be complicated by circumstances beyond a hunter's control (war, pestilence, Montezuma's Revenge). Should the portal close before the hunter has found it, he or she risks being trapped in the past forever. I am in the process of developing a device that will sniff out any portal in the vicinity and, in the absence of a strong unfavourable breeze, I trust it will be a satisfactory solution to the problem.

Such a system will require the portal to emit either a clear smell signal or selection of charged particles.

The Smell Signal

Word hunters on missions to or close to Sumatra, Indonesia, were requested to bring back seeds of the foulest-smelling plant in nature, the bunga bangkai or corpse flower. Producing an odour like rotting meat, the dark red flower even heats up to human body temperature to better spread its stench. The plant's putrid stink and meat-like appearance attract the flies and flesh-eating beetles needed to pollinate it.

Seeds were obtained by Emmeline Hunter in 1911. Since then, Caractacus's work has been ongoing, to breed a tiny version of the corpse flower that might grow at each portal, and to refine the portal sniffer's sensing apparatus.

Ketchup - Emmeline Hunter

~E~ HUNTER

1727 - first ketchup recipe in English, in Eliza Smith's 'The Compleat Housewife'. (Her ketchup ingredients included anchovies, shallots, vinegar, white wine, cloves, ginger, mace, nutmeg, pepper and lemon peel. No tomatoes appeared in ketchup for another century.)

Emmeline

1711 - first appearance in English in Charles Lockyer's 'An Account of the Trade in India': 'Soy comes in Tubbs from Jappan, and the best Ketchup from Tonquin; yet good of both sorts are made and sold very cheap in China.'

1690 - 'catchup' appears in 'Dictionary of the Canting Crew'.

1340s - 'kichap' in Malay (my chance to foray to Sumatra to bring back the seeds of that infernal stink plant).

1280s - 'koechiap' meaning fish brine, from the Changchew dialect of Chinese.

Now known as Zhangzhou dialect
— Alan Hunter

Ripening

To ensure prompt and timely ripening of the corpse flower, the most readily available substance is pythian vapour.

For later hunters, see olefiant gas or ethylene.

The best sources of pythian vapor in Britain, during the time of English, are ripe apples and pears, though a later arrival, the banana, is superior to both.   Montagu

Conclusion: After 1633, all devices to be fitted with a ripe or overripe banana by word hunters before leaving home. Earlier devices, that is devices preceding the arrival of the banana in England in 1633, to use an apple or pear.

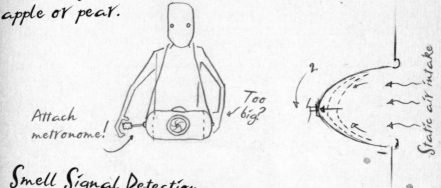

Attach metronome!

Too big?

2.

Static air intake

Smell Signal Detection

With the aid of a hand pump, the nasotube draws the air past a crystal of olfactorium, which darkens dramatically in the presence of a certain combination of odours. This darkening reduces the passage of light to the light meter, giving a numerical reading of intensity. Readings from different directions combine to make the porta-compass needle point towards the direction of the portal.

Electrostatic Signal Detection

When the portal is activated, so too is its micro-storm generator, which injects warm, moist air into a pool of cold air to produce a micro-thunderstorm. The lightning generated from this changes the air's molecular structures and charges (creating ozone, etc). The hand pump draws air to operate a miniature turbine, which generates the magnetic field required to draw the molecules into the device (with their flow towards the device also assisted by the pump — genius, no?). A needle indicates the direction of the portal.

Note 1: It is essential that the pump be operated at precisely the right frequency for the portal. An aid to managing pumping speed will be provided.

Note 2: May be misleading during actual thunderstorms, when air in any direction could be identified as a portal (hence the expression 'any portal in a storm').

What's that Stink? by Al

Analysis of the stink components of the bunga bangkai or corpse flower.

Dimethyl trisulfide — limburger cheese
Trimethylamine — rotting fish
Isovaleric acid — sweaty socks
Indole — mothballs
Dimethyl disulfide — Lexi Hunter's breath (aka garlic)

Portal Sniffer Trial Notes

Report by: Mursili
Word hunters: Lexi, Al, Alan and Mursili (2016)

While we are all very excited that this device has finally reached trial stage after many years of development, it is another prototype we hope will decrease in size … Use of the sniffer (smell mode) is not without its challenges. While we were hunting 'fork' in 1430 (first appearance of a table fork, in an inventory for a dining hall), the pig being fattened for the banquet ate the banana. Unfortunately, we lost the peel, though it will surely decompose and cause no problem.

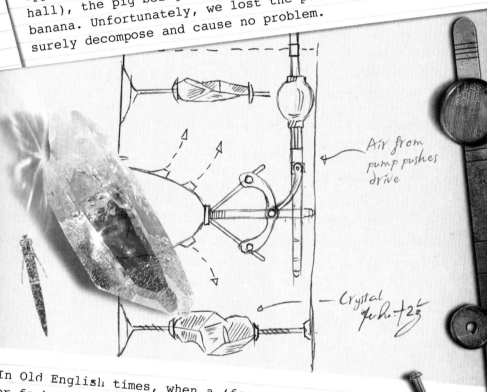

Air from pump pushes drive

— Crystal
Feb. 25

In Old English times, when a 'forca' was a pitchfork or forked weapon, we located a pear and used it with some success. The pear continued with us back to the fork's Latin origins ('furca'), though I noticed a few rat-sized bites had been taken from it. While the sniffer correctly indicated the direction of the portal, hunters felt that adding a search for appropriate fruit would sometimes be a bigger issue than the search for the portal itself.

Cleopatra's Sweet Sesame Honey Balls

(DULCIS SESAMUM)

Two pieces of papyrus blew into my robe on our way into the Library of Alexandria during the fire in 48BC. Interestingly, most of the writing was in Latin, rather than Egyptian. So I wondered what they were about ...

Ingredientae

- 1 libra siligo-inis
- 1 quarterivs aqva
- 1 septvnx ficvs
- 1 septvnx dactylvs
- 1 septvnx ivglans
- 1 triens coccora
- 1 dodrans mellis

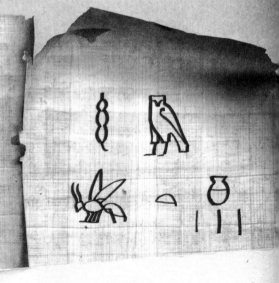

Looks like ingredients for a recipe — translation on next page.

Al

Caractacus, I have taken the liberty of translating the second piece of papyrus. It appears to be from Apollodorus of Sicily and reads as such:

On the orders of my Queen, I shall bring her to you in the night in the palace of Ptolemy in Alexandria. We shall come by sea, in the first night hours. We have a disguise planned, which I shall not risk putting into words. Should you wish to prepare to welcome her, I can assure you she appreciates the dulcis (cocorra) here described.

'Coccora' appears to refer to seeds. Seeds in general or a seed to which I can find no recent references? Likely to have used sesame seeds in some versions. Coccum – cocci – coccora? Scarlet berry? Dye from scarlet berry? Seed from scarlet berry?

Scarlet berries by Al

Timeline of 'Sesame'

1435 in English

1355 Middle French 'sisame'

110 BC Latin 'sesamum'

512 BC Doric Greek 'sasamon'

580 BC Late Babylonian
'shawash-shammu'
(meaning oil seed)

Harriet Hunter (1710)

EARLS·IMAGES
LONDON·IRELAND

Caractacus, here is the recipe using the metric system. It actually works! I did the mixing and rolling, and Grandad did the frying.

Al

300g flour

150mL water

200g chopped dried figs

200g chopped dates

200g chopped walnuts

100g sesame seeds

250mL honey

Balls should be about this big when rolled

Mix flour and water and add dried fruits and nuts.

Shape and roll into small balls (makes about 32).

Roll balls in sesame seeds. Simmer 125mL honey in frying pan. Place half of the balls in frying pan, rolling around and cooking for about five minutes as the honey caramelises. Remove balls and place on baking paper to cool. Simmer another 125mL honey and cook the remaining balls.

- The honey forms a foam that gets darker as you cook.

- Take the balls out while the honey is still brown, and make sure it doesn't turn black.

- Be VERY CAREFUL when frying the balls (it 'requires adult supervision', as so many fun things in life do). The simmering honey can easily burn your skin.

- Clean the caramelised honey residue quickly from the pan, tongs, etc, since it sets pretty hard.

These are not dried figs. DOUG!!

Not bad, but would be better with chocolate.
Lexi

Yeah, right, but chocolate was not known in this part of the world for another 1500 YEARS!!
Al

Anti-Nausea Device

Record made by my own hand, Caractacus, 498AD,
with the aid of certain hunters - work in progress

Dark Ages nausea remains a problem for word
hunters. I shall keep preparing my queasy water tonic
according to the current formula, even though some
hunters take time to respond to it. While my pigs seem
fond of hunters arriving and vomiting, it does get in
the way of doing business. So, a device is needed to
allow hunters to arrive in the fifth century
nausea-free. Work towards a prototype anti-nausea
helmet follows, incorporating leading technologies
from a range of civilisations and times.

Note from Will Hunter (1918), chasing 'tycoon'

Chinese doctors have identified a point on the forearm where they apply pressure to relieve nausea, using a finger, or a pearl or button attached to a strap. The point lies a distance they call 'two tsoon' (about the width of four fingers) above the wrist creases on the palm side of the arm. The Chinese also use ginger for nausea relief, sometimes chewing it, or taking it as a tea or powder, or even inhaling the fragrance.

Here

'Tycoon' came into English in 1857 meaning important person, from Japanese 'taikun' meaning great lord or prince, from Chinese 'tai' – great – and 'kiun' – lord.

Will H

GINGER

Alan Hunter (1983): use of 'tycoon' to apply to a wealthy person in business is from soon after Will's time.

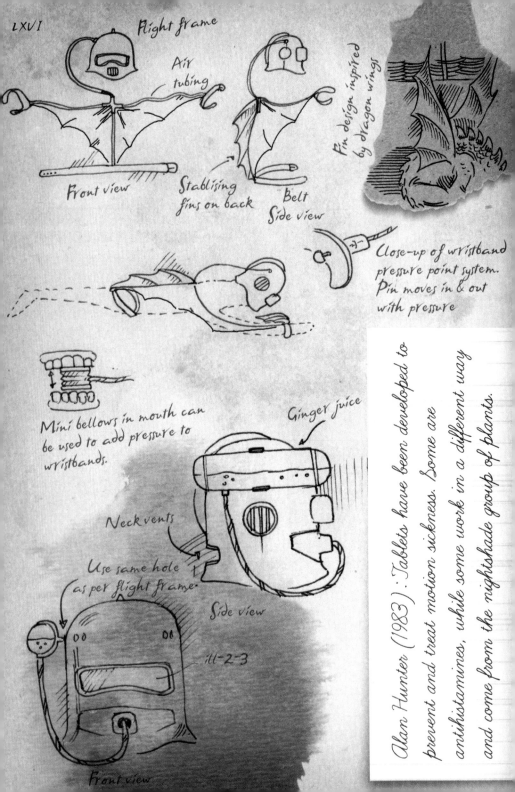

LXVI

Flight frame

Air tubing

Fin design inspired by dragon wings

Front view

Stablising fins on back

Belt
Side view

Close-up of wristband pressure point system. Pin moves in & out with pressure

Mini bellows in mouth can be used to add pressure to wristbands.

Ginger juice

Neck vents

Use same hole as per flight frame

ill-2-3

Side view

Front view

Alan Hunter (1983): Tablets have been developed to prevent and treat motion sickness. Some are antihistamines, while some work in a different way and come from the nightshade group of plants.

Try to block visual inputs showing motion. Limit fields of vision. Is there any way of using the sailors' trick of staring at the horizon? A falling hunter has no horizon.

MAKE A HORIZON.

Ill-2 Goggles

Oil and water level to steady eyes and keep track of which way is up.

Yes, yes, please do something about the Dark Ages vomiting. I've been setting a big Google on this one. There's some promising research from NASA, the space people, into shutter glasses. The shutters need to shut for 10 milliseconds at a time, four to eight times each second. Possible? Please?

Mursili

Ill-3 option

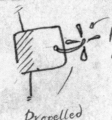

Fan on front of goggles to create strobe lighting. Has been known to ease nausea.

Propelled by wind

The model like a diver's helmet is about the size of our entire backpacks and looks like it'd weigh at least 10kg. Any idea how we might be able to carry it? Could you try making one that'd fit in a pocket? Does it come in pink?

Lexi

(2013): Now available as patches that you put behind your ear.

Al

Okay, you guys. (See what I did there?) Once again we hunters require your skills in documenting our brave word-saving journey, so sharpen your styluses and get writing/drawing!

YiW,
Mursili

WORD QUEST

GUY:

man, person, in plural can refer to groups of men and/or women (current use from Am Eng, ultimately from PGerm 'Wido')

1847 — 'guy' takes on the meaning of fellow (used in American English)

1836 — 'guy' refers to a very badly or grotesquely dressed person (used in British English)

1806 — effigy of Guy Fawkes burned on Bonfire Night in Britain, the anniversary of his attempt to blow up the Houses of Parliament in what became known as the Gunpowder Plot

& MORE

1605 — Guy Fawkes brings his name into disrepute when he's caught guarding several barrels of gunpowder in a cellar under the British Houses of Parliament in an attempt to assassinate the King of Great Britain

1066 — the Normans bring the name 'Guy' to England

before 600 — 'Guy' begins as the Germanic name 'Wido'

'**P** GERM,' LEXI SAID when Al showed her the word pulsing with light in the dictionary. 'Is that Proto-Germanic again?'

'Yes, but it doesn't always mean needing to fight Romans.' It had so far, Al thought, and he knew that was on Lexi's mind too. 'We can't let "guy" get lost. It's too useful.'

He held out the dictionary so that Lexi could activate the '& more' button. She already had her backpack on. They were both as prepared as they could be.

Lexi pressed the button. The floor shuddered. The window swung open and mist blew in. And they were falling.

They hit unseen bumps in the fog, coming too fast to count. When the fog parted they were over a city, smoke from factories blowing across it, a familiar river ahead of them.

'London.' Lexi said it first.

Nineteenth-century London, Al thought, from the size and the amount of industry. A big dirty city, not a battlefield. But why were they landing in London for an American word?

Lexi and Al fell towards the river and then to the north of it, between the City and the parliament, and then towards a narrow street lined by grimy brick buildings four storeys high.

'Aargh,' Lexi said as her lungs were suddenly sucked in and bound. 'Not another corset!'

She landed with a wicker basket in her hand – again. She'd ended up with one twice when they'd hunted 'dollar', and plenty of other times. They were such annoying things to carry around. Meanwhile Al, as usual, had a much more practical leather satchel over one shoulder. He was wearing a short jacket with matching trousers, a waistcoat and a

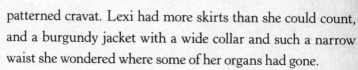

patterned cravat. Lexi had more skirts than she could count, and a burgundy jacket with a wide collar and such a narrow waist she wondered where some of her organs had gone.

'So sick of the past and its unfair dress codes,' Lexi said, attempting a twirl to show that it wasn't possible. 'But don't worry. It's all good as long as I don't need to breathe.'

'Children!' a man's voice boomed. 'This is no place for young folk of the better classes.'

The man had a neat moustache, a knee-length coat, a waistcoat and a cravat quite like Al's. But what grabbed Al's attention more was the two men behind him, who were in navy uniforms, with top hats, and belts that each carried a wooden truncheon and a rattle.

Al had his hand in his satchel. He thought he could feel five pegs, no, six. Among the words they hunted, six-peggers were rare. One of the pegs would be activated, showing the date, but now wasn't the time to pull it out. He could guess though. He knew from one of his history books that London's police force had been set up in 1829.

'Charles Collette,' the man introduced himself. 'Society for the Suppression of Vice. You two should head back to the Strand. The books stocked here aren't for you. They aren't for any of us with a shred of decency, with their crude drawings of a person's private parts, and biological information we need to keep from the working classes.'

Lexi started to laugh, but quickly turned it into a cough.

'We hear Mr Dugdale has a new book he's about to publish.' Charles nodded in the direction of a bookshop, one of several on the street.

'Dugdale? But the store's sign says "H. Smith",' Al said.

'We've already shut him down as "D. Brown" and "J. Turner",' one of the police officers replied, 'but it's always just Dirty Dugdale.'

'And this time we have a further reason to investigate,' Charles Collette added. 'This new book, by all accounts, has been compiled by one Renton Nicholson, purveyor of bawdy entertainments. And he has the gall to write as "Lord Chief Baron", as though with some authority, while thieving the private satirical work of the Earl of Ellesmere as the basis of it.'

'We hear Nicholson's added spicy engravings,' the police officer said, sounding rather more interested than he should be. 'And accounts of lewd happenings.'

'Yes.' Charles frowned at him. 'And to make it look less like the Earl's work, he's written the new material in modern language. American language, some of it.' He said the last part as if that was the worst of it.

'American language,' Lexi said, nudging Al with her elbow. 'Goodness me.'

They needed to see that book. They both knew it. Somewhere, behind the darkened windows of H. Smith's bookshop, was the word 'guy' on a printed page, ready to be spoken, to activate the portal.

The police raid was about to start, and somehow they had to be part of it.

Nick,
Why did you stop?!
That story was just
getting interesting…
Terry

What We've Found Out About the word 'Guy'

Today the word 'guy' is so widespread it's hard to imagine it wasn't always part of English. When it's singular, it's still more commonly used to refer to a male person, but when plural (for example, 'you guys') gender doesn't come into it. That pattern really developed in the US in the 1970s, though the first record of a woman being referred to as a guy is in a letter by the American playwright Eugene O'Neill in 1927: 'She's a "real guy". You'd like her immensely.' Not long after, in 1932, the journal 'American Speech' records one girl saying to her female friends, 'Come on, guys' - something that sounds very 21st century.

'Guy' had once been a very judgemental word, but it lost that connection in the US in the 19th century, as Guy Fawkes references were not recognised as much there. Interestingly, the earliest written use of that version of 'guy' is in a book from the late 1840s about the seamy side of London nightlife, 'The Swell's Night Guide', which refers to 'a rich old Guy' and was the work of a publisher who temporarily went by the name 'H. Smith'...

And what about the earlier British meaning? It was far from flattering. In 1836 Julia Maitland wrote in a letter, 'The gentlemen are all "rigged tropical" ... grisly guys some of them turn out!' For Julia, a 'guy' was someone luridly and disturbingly dressed.

THE NEW
SWELL'S
NIGHT GUIDE
BEAUTIFULLY ILLUSTRATED.
PRICE ONE SHILLING.

That association with unusual attire probably came from the way people dressed up their 'guys' - effigies of Guy Fawkes made by stuffing old clothes with straw - which were burnt on British Bonfire Night every 5th November. The tradition of bonfires on 5th November goes back to the failed Gunpowder Plot of 1605, though the burning of guys came much later. Guy Fawkes was part of a Catholic militant group who wanted to assassinate the Protestant king by blowing up the British Houses of Parliament to restore a Catholic monarch to the throne. When the plot was foiled, Londoners lit bonfires to celebrate the king's survival. This was soon followed by the passing of the 'Observance of 5th November Act', marking the day as an official celebration.

That takes 'guy' back as far as Guy Fawkes, but what about the earlier use of the name? We know 'Guy' is one of many names that came to England with the Normans and that it is descended from the much older 'Wido', though no one seems to know precisely when or how it evolved.

WORD QUEST

by Al Hunter

'wido' might have a connection with the Proto-Germanic 'widu' meaning wood, and might have been a name given to someone who lived near a wood. It's perhaps more likely that it comes from the Proto-Germanic 'witanan' meaning to guard. This became the Frankish 'witan', which became 'guier' and then 'guider' in Old French, leading to both the word 'guide' in Middle English and the Italian first name Guido. Maybe they also directly led to 'Guy'?

WORD QUEST

Interestingly, there's another Guy Fawkes connection. Guy fought for Spain in the Eighty Years' War against the Dutch, and in 1603 unsuccessfully urged the Spanish King Philip II to support a Catholic rebellion in England. While in Spain, he actually changed his name to Guido!

Terry,
Who wouldn't want to finish writing that story? Bonfires, a fiendish plot and yet another chance to fight the Battle of Hastings as the Normans bring 'Guy' to England! Start writing, kids!

Nick

P.S. For anyone thinking of complaining about me calling young people 'kids', we've been doing that in English since the 1590s!

PENNY FOR THE GUY

WORDS WE COULDN'T SAVE

By Al Hunter

Let's face it, despite our best efforts, many words have disappeared from the English language. I wanted to try to change that. Sometimes, when we travel to the past to hunt — and save — a word, we come across other words we've never heard before. Since these may become lost later, I write them down and make notes about their meanings. But the turbulence of time travel sometimes jumbles them up in my backpack — and in my head! I've matched some of these excellent words with their meanings again, but I'd love some help with the rest. And, of course, I'd like help bringing them back to life too!

Pigsney

a term of endearment

Uhtceare

a feeling of anxiety about the day ahead, waking the sufferer before dawn and preventing them from going back to sleep

Wamblecropt

to be overcome with nausea or indigestion

someone who refuses to give up old ideas even though they've been proven wrong

Mumpsimus

Callipygian

having attractively shaped buttocks

Curglaff

the shock felt when plunging into seriously cold water

Fudgel

creating the impression of doing work while actually doing nothing

5 Groke

8 Slubberdegullion

2 Scurryfunge

3 Feague

6 Snecklifter

7 Jargogle

Cockalorum

4

1 Snollygoster

F to jumble or confuse

D hurried house cleaning done in the time between seeing a neighbour and that neighbour arriving at the door

B to stare at someone who's eating in the hope that they'll share their food with you

H a short person with a high opinion of themselves

G to put ginger or a live eel up a horse's bottom to make the horse seem more active

C someone who looks in through a pub doorway to see if there's anyone inside likely to buy them a drink

A a seriously messy person, perhaps even slobbering

E a cunning person who will sacrifice principles to get what they want (particularly applied to politicians)

Nick and Terry,

I am sure that, as Men of Words, you know all of these and use them regularly. If you need a little refresher, I have inscribed the answers on page 80 of this notebook.

Yours in Some Really Interesting Words,
Mursili

Correspondence Received
Regarding Credentials

Terry Whidborne
Illustrator

Hi Mursili,
Thanks for requesting more information on my background. I've been working in advertising in Brisbane for some time and actually met Nick during a TV commercial shoot. He was the main star. How funny is that! We've kept in contact ever since and even climbed a glacier together.

Along with my own interest in words, I also love to illustrate. I've been creating illustrations for some time now and the Word Hunters novels were my first published books.

I'm currently working on a few other books and also some online world projects that inspire writers. I'm in the process of writing my own novella too.

Yours in Words (and Pictures),

Terry

Nick Earls
Author

Mursili,
Thanks for your enquiry into my background. Was the criminal history check really necessary? What chance have I had to commit a crime while I've been sitting here writing 26 books (two of which have become films and five have become plays)?

I can vouch for Terry too. Very trustworthy. For example, he's telling the truth when he says we met doing a TV campaign promoting Brisbane. Terry made it all go really smoothly. I got a straw with some warm green drink in it up my nose, a dart in my leg and a cockatoo swore at me. Clearly you've picked the right team.

Nick

P.S. When Terry says 'first published books', he means published in the agreed sense of 'hidden in a vault guarded by a python', so there's no problem there. Your secrets are safe with us.

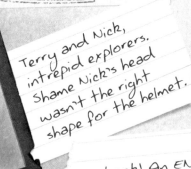

Terry and Nick, intrepid explorers. Shame Nick's head wasn't the right shape for the helmet.

Look! An ENORMOUS gold medal given to Nick for a book he wrote. He must be very good!
Mursili

Nick and Terry,

Disaster! Look what I found a child carrying at Cubberla Creek State School after your visit! A kind of advertising perhaps? It appears something has gone terribly wrong with the UQP vault and python! Someone has stolen crucial word hunters material and turned it into books with your names on them!! The fact that these books are quite brilliant only makes the situation worse, since they will no doubt be read far and wide! Our secrets are secrets no more!

What are we to do???

Yours in Wordless Panic,
Mursili

NICK EARLS &
TERRY WHIDBORNE

The thrilling conclusion
to an action-packed
adventure series for the
word nerd in us all.

Terry has come a long way
since his entry for the
Dr Who Dalek drawing
competition when he was 8.
Standards weren't too high,
I take it. M

First published 2016 by University of Queensland Press
PO Box 6042, St Lucia, Queensland 4067 Australia

www.uqp.com.au • uqp@uqp.uq.edu.au

Cubberla Creek School Library

Typeset and internal design by Terry Whidborne,
except text design of Word Quests by Jo Hunt
Colour reproduction by Splitting Image
Printed in China by 1010 Asia Printing Limited

Cataloguing-in-Publication Data
National Library of Australia

Earls, Nick, 1963– author.
Word hunters : top secret files / Nick Earls ;
Terry Whidborne, illustrator,.

ISBN 978 0 7022 5402 4 (pbk).

For children.

Encyclopedias and dictionaries--Juvenile fiction.
English language--Obsolete words--Juvenile fiction.
Adventure stories.
Children's stories.

Whidborne, Terry, illustrator.

A823.3

University of Queensland Press uses papers that are natural,
renewable and recyclable products made from wood grown in
sustainable forests. The logging and manufacturing processes
conform to the environmental regulations of the country of origin.

The publisher recommends all activities and recipes in this book
be undertaken with adult supervision.

ANSWERS

All at Sea in Ancient Phoenicia Byblos: ∠ ≤ ⅂ Sidon: ꝿ ⅂Ⱶ Carthage: ⅹ ⱳ ⅆ Ɓ ⅹ ⅑Φ Tyre: ⅑ Ⳃⳁ Leptis Magna: ꝗ Φ ⱳ ∠ Algiers: ꝗ ⱳ ⅹ ꝗ Ibiza: ⱳ ⅂ ⱳ ꝗ Cadiz: ꝗ ⟨ ⅑ ⅄   The blue route is the correct one.

Words We Couldn't Save 1 = E: 2 = D: 3 = G: 4 = H: 5 = B: 6 = C: 7 = F: 8 = A.

& MORE

MURSILI

GRANDAD AL

AL